You do not necessarily need to a two-hundred pound man to become a bodybuilder – you do not never need to spend five days a week in the gym! All you need is the motivation and the desire to change your body for the better. If you want to improve your fitness and build a better body, this book is the perfect place to start.

In this book you will learn about bodybuilding at its most basic level including general information about what bodybuilding is and which bodybuilding programs are known for producing the best results. You will receive an introduction to the three core principles of bodybuilding as well as tips for bulking and cutting. Most importantly, however, you will learn about nutrition for bodybuilding including tips regarding what to eat and when.

So, if you are ready to experience the challenge of bodybuilding, keep reading!

# Table of Contents

Introduction ................................................................... 9

    Important Terms to Know ................................... 11

Chapter One: What is Bodybuilding? ............................ 15

    1. Introduction to Bodybuilding ........................... 16

    2. History of Bodybuilding .................................. 19

    3. Popular Bodybuilding Programs ...................... 23

        a. The 5x5 Program .......................................... 23

        b. German Volume Training ............................. 24

        c. The FST-7 Program ...................................... 24

        d. Upper/Lower Split Training ......................... 25

        e. Full Body Workout Program ........................ 25

Chapter Two: The Three Core Principles ....................... 27

    1. Smart Training ................................................ 28

        a. The Process of Muscle Growth .................... 28

        b. Tips for Training Correctly .......................... 30

    2. Quality Nutrition ............................................. 32

    3. Adequate Rest ................................................. 36

Chapter Three: Bulking and Cutting ............................. 39

    1. When to Bulk and When to Cut ....................... 40

    2. Calculating Calorie Intake ............................... 44

        a. Calculating Calorie Maintenance Level ....... 45

b. Calculating Bulking Calorie Level ..........................47

c. Calculating Cutting Calorie Level............................47

3. Macronutrient Ratios ......................................................49

Chapter Four: Nutrition for Bodybuilding .......................53

1. Diet Tips to Burn Fat ......................................................54

2. Nutrition Tips for Building Muscle ............................57

3. Nutrition Myths and Mistakes to Avoid ....................60

Chapter Five: What to Eat and When ................................65

1. Pre-Workout Nutrition ..................................................66

2. During Workout Nutrition............................................67

3. Post-Workout Nutrition..................................................69

Chapter Six: Fat-Burning Recipes for Cutting ..................71

1. Breakfast Recipes ............................................................72

    Tomato Basil Egg White Omelet ..................................73

    Cinnamon Steel-Cut Oats ...............................................74

    Spinach and Mushroom Frittata...................................75

    Cottage Cheese Breakfast Parfait .................................76

    Sautéed Sweet Potato Hash............................................77

    Herbed Spinach Egg White Omelet ............................78

    Yogurt and Fresh Berry Parfait.....................................79

2. Snacks and Green Smoothies .......................................80

    Cottage Cheese Crackers with Smoked Salmon ......81

Easy Green Tea Smoothie ............................................. 82

Spinach Parmesan Snack Muffins ............................. 83

Banana Oatmeal Smoothie ......................................... 84

Baked Oatmeal Muffins ............................................... 85

Spinach Green Apple Smoothie .................................. 86

3. Entrée Recipes ............................................................. 87

Mediterranean-Style Tuna Salad ............................... 88

Almond-Crusted Baked Halibut ................................ 89

Creamy Carrot Ginger Soup ....................................... 90

Slow Cooker Turkey Sloppy Joes ............................... 91

Balsamic Glazed Grilled Salmon ............................... 92

Spinach Salad with Green Apples .............................. 93

Chapter Seven: Muscle-Building Recipes for Bulking .... 94

1. Breakfast Recipes ........................................................ 94

Corned Beef Hash with Fried Eggs ........................... 96

Easy Spanish Omelet .................................................... 98

Sausage and Egg Breakfast Casserole ....................... 99

Apple Cinnamon Breakfast Quinoa ........................ 100

Ham and Cheese Egg Muffins .................................. 101

2. Snacks and Protein Shakes ..................................... 102

Avocado Deviled Eggs ............................................... 103

Tropical Fruit Protein Shake ..................................... 104

Cottage Cheese Veggie Dip ..................................................105

Peanut Butter Banana Protein Shake ......................106

Spiced Mixed Nuts ..................................................107

Chocolate Covered Strawberry Shake .....................108

Peanut Butter Protein Cookies .................................109

Berries and Cream Protein Shake ............................110

3. Entrée Recipes ..................................................111

Rosemary Roasted Chicken Breasts ........................112

Curried Red Lentil Stew .........................................113

Coconut-Crusted Halibut Fillets .............................115

Soy-Marinated Flank Steak .....................................116

Spicy Beef and Double Bean Chili ..........................117

Apple-Roasted Turkey Breast ..................................119

Conclusion ..................................................121

Index ..................................................123

References ..................................................131

# Introduction

When you hear the word "bodybuilder" you probably picture a giant, muscle-bound man with bulging veins and artificially tanned skin. While this image may be accurate for some bodybuilders, it is a stereotype that many fitness enthusiasts do not fit into. In fact, you can be a bodybuilder without ever picking up a pair of dumbbells. The simplest definition of a bodybuilder is simply someone who wants to build a better body.

Building a better body is not something you can achieve overnight and it is generally not something that happens by accident. In order to improve your body composition and your fitness, you need to be intentional about what you eat

# Introduction

and when you eat on top of following an exercise regimen. There is a science to bodybuilding if you really want to get serious about it, but you can still reap the benefits of bodybuilding without allowing it to completely take over your life.

In this book you will learn about bodybuilding at its most basic level. Here you will find general information about what bodybuilding is and which bodybuilding programs are known for producing the best results. You will receive an introduction to the three core principles of bodybuilding as well as tips for bulking and cutting. Most importantly, however, you will learn about nutrition for bodybuilding including tips regarding what to eat and when. To help you achieve your bodybuilding goals, you will also receive a collection of recipes to get you started. So, if you are ready to experience the challenge of bodybuilding, keep reading!

# Introduction

## *Important Terms to Know*

**Abduction** – Moving a limb away from the center of the body; such as lifting the arm.

**Adduction** – Moving a limb toward the center of the body; such as bringing a lifted arm down.

**Aerobic Exercise** – A type of prolonged, moderate-intensity exercise that expends oxygen levels in the muscle at or below the level at which it is being replenished. Ex: running, swimming, walking.

**Anabolic Steroid** – A synthetic chemical that mimics the muscle-building characteristics of testosterone – leads to bigger gains in muscle.

**Barbell** – A weight consisting of a handle with metal discs at either end.

**Bench Press** – A chest exercise done from a seated position or lying on a bench.

**Body Composition** – The percentage of total bodyweight composed of fat versus lean muscle tissue.

**Bulking** – Gaining body weight by adding muscle and/or body fat.

# Introduction

**Cardiovascular Training** – Type of physical training that strengthens the heart and blood vessels. <u>Ex</u>: running.

**Circuit Training** – Moving quickly from one exercise to another to keep the pulse rate high.

**Cutting** – The practice of restricting calorie intake to lose body fat.

**Dead Lift** – An exercise that involves lifting the weight off the floor to weight height while standing erect; strengthens the lower back.

**Failure** – The point at which the muscles become so fatigued that you physically cannot complete another rep.

**Intensity** – The relative degree of effort put into each set during your workout.

**Lean Body Mass** – Everything in the body except for fat – this includes muscle, bone, organs, skin and nails.

**Mass** – The relative size of each muscle group.

**Metabolic Rate** – The rate at which your body converts stored energy into working energy.

**Military Press** – An exercise that involves pressing a barbell from the upper chest; completed in a standing or sitting position.

# Introduction

**Olympic Barbell** – A type of barbell used for exercises such as squats, bench press, and deadlifts; weighs 45 pounds.

**Power Lifts** – The three exercises used in powerlifting competition; squat, deadlift and bench press.

**Repetition (Rep)** – The number of times you perform an exercise in one set.

**Resistance Exercise** – Exercises using weights or bodyweight to resist force. Ex: dumbbell curls or push-ups.

**Routine** – The total list of exercises, sets, and repetitions used during a single training session; also called a program.

**Set** – A group of repetitions of a single exercise performed before taking a rest period.

**Spotter** – A person who stands by to offer help if needed during a specific exercise.

**Squat** – A leg exercise performed in a standing position that involves bending the knees to lift a barbell.

**Strength Training** – The use of resistance weight training to build muscle.

**Workout** – A bodybuilding or weight training session.

# Introduction

Diet and Nutrition for Bodybuilding

# Chapter One: What is Bodybuilding?

Bodybuilding looks different for each person who calls themselves a bodybuilder. For some, it may involve daily weight lifting sessions while, for others, if may consist of healthy eating and regular physical activity. In this chapter you will receive an introduction to bodybuilding including some of the potential benefits. You will also receive a history of bodybuilding as well as some information about popular training programs.

## Chapter One: What is Bodybuilding?

## *1. Introduction to Bodybuilding*

There are many who would argue that bodybuilding is not a sport but there are many athletes who engage in bodybuilding. The simplest definition for the term "bodybuilder" is "someone who builds a better body". This can be accomplished through a variety of means including following a healthy diet, engaging in regular exercise, and sculpting the muscles through weight lifting routines. You do not necessarily need to compete in bodybuilding competitions in order to be a bodybuilder. In fact, you can become a bodybuilder without setting foot inside a gym – there are plenty of at-home workouts available.

Bodybuilding is a large and varied industry because there is no set definition for what makes a body better. For some people, a better body is one with a low body fat percentage and a high level of endurance. For someone else, a better body is one with a high percentage of lean muscle mass. In many cases, people engage in bodybuilding not just as a means of improving their physical appearance, but as a means of challenging themselves to attain ever loftier goals for fitness and physique.

Though bodybuilding takes many different forms, anyone who engages in bodybuilding has the potential to reap certain benefits. <u>Some of the many benefits of</u>

# Chapter One: What is Bodybuilding?

bodybuilding include:

- Decreased risk for heart disease due to increased cardiovascular endurance.

- Reduced cholesterol and blood pressure due to regular exercise.

- Increased strength in bones and joints – reduced risk for injury or arthritis.

- Reduction in stress, anxiety, depression and other mood problems.

- Increase in self-esteem and confidence levels as well as positive self-image.

- Increased blood flow to the brain – improved cognitive performance, decreased risk for cognitive decline.

- Improved oxygen levels – good for brain function and total-body health.

- Encourages healthy eating habits and improved nutrition.

- Increased lean muscle mass, lower body fat percentage.

These are just a few of the many benefits associated with improved physical fitness – you do not necessarily need to lift weights five days a week to obtain these benefits. The more physically fit you become, the more benefits you will receive. Becoming physically fit involves more than just lifting weights – it is also about nutrition. You can lift all the weights you want but unless you fuel your body properly you won't see any growth. The food you eat before, during and after a workout will have a direct impact on the results of your training. You will learn more about this concept later in this book.

## 2. History of Bodybuilding

The tradition of stone lifting can be traced all the way back to ancient Egypt and Greece, though weight lifting didn't come into popularity in the Western world until the 1800s. Around 1880, strongmen came into being, known for displaying various feats of strength for the public and challenging each other in competitions. Strength was the focus of strongmen - not body composition and physique like modern bodybuilders - so many strongmen had round stomachs and fatty limbs.

The practice of bodybuilding developed during the late 1800s and it was promoted in England by the so-called

## Chapter One: What is Bodybuilding?

"Father of Modern Bodybuilding", Eugen Sandow. Sandow himself trained hard and entertained audiences with feats of strength – he also played a role in creating some of the first bodybuilding exhibitions. Sandow built a stage where he and other strongmen competed in strength demonstrations and wrestling matches. In 1936, a music film called *The Great Ziegfeld* as shot, depicting the beginnings of modern bodybuilding.

So great was Sandow's success that he capitalized on his fame, creating several businesses for himself. Sandow is credited with the invention of some of the first exercise equipment including machined dumbbells, tension bands, and spring pulleys. Before long, Sandow's body became the standard of ideal body proportions and other bodybuilders were judged based on how closely they matched Sandow's proportions.

The first large-scale bodybuilding competition occurred on September 14, 1901 and it was named the "Great Competition". This competition was held in the Royal Albert Hall in London and was judged by Sandow himself along with Sir Arthur Conan Doyle and Sir Charles Lawes. The contest drew a large crowd – in fact, the crowd was so large that many people had to be turned away. Prizes were awarded for first, second, and third place winners.

## Chapter One: What is Bodybuilding?

In January 1904, the first bodybuilding competition in America took place at Madison Square Garden in New York City. Al Treloar was the winner of the competition and he was named "The Most Perfectly Developed Man in the World" in addition to winning a cash prize of $1,000. Following the win, Thomas Edison made a film of Treloar's posing routine just as he had made films of Sandow's routine several years earlier. These were the first three films to feature a bodybuilder.

Bodybuilding really began to gain popularity in the United States during the 1950s and 1950s as muscle training became more commonplace. Notable athletes and gymnastic champions began competing for titles like Mr. Universe and Mr. America and more bodybuilders came to be featured in films. Steve Reeves played the role of Hercules and Reg Park became famous for his role as Samson. Various other bodybuilders made appearances on popular television series like *The Monkees* and *The Beverly Hillbillies*.

By the 1970s, famous bodybuilders like Arnold Schwarzenegger and Franco Columbu had stepped onto the scene and the International Federation of Bodybuilding and Fitness (IFBB) dominated the competitive bodybuilding industry. It was also during this time that there was a rise in anabolic steroid used by bodybuilders and pro-level bodybuilders began to attain sizes never before seen. This spurred the IFBB to introduce doping tests for steroids as well as other banned substances in competition.

During the early 2000s, the IFBB sought to make bodybuilding an Olympic sport. The organization did obtain IOC membership, but bodybuilding as never added as a full contest. Modern bodybuilders can still compete and there are many different levels of bodybuilding competitions. Professional bodybuilders are those who won qualifying competitions as amateurs and thus earned a pro card from one of the bodybuilding organizations. These members then have the right to compete for monetary prizes – they may also receive compensation from sponsors.

## 3. Popular Bodybuilding Programs

When it comes to choosing a bodybuilding program you have the option of creating your own routine or of following a set program. To give you an idea what a bodybuilding program looks like, consider the following five programs:

- The 5x5 Program
- German Volume Training
- The FST-7 Program
- Upper/Lower Split Training
- Full Body Workout Program

**a. The 5x5 Program**

This program is a great place for beginners to start because it is very easy to follow – it also offers excellent potential for gaining strength and size. The 5x5 program consists of three main exercises, each targeting one of the main muscle groups. All you do is perform five sets of five repetitions – you can increase the weight with each set, if you want to speed up your gains. When following this program you should plan to work out every other day, alternating between two sets of exercises. You also have the option of adding isolated muscle exercises to your plan.

## b. German Volume Training

This training program is very similar to the 5x5 program except that you will be performing more sets and more repetitions during each set. During each workout you select one compound exercise for each of your main muscle groups then perform 10 sets of 10 repetitions. At the end of the workout you can add some isolation exercises, but only do 2 to 3 sets of 10 to 15 repetitions each. The benefit of this program over the 5x5 program is that you can build muscle very quickly, as long as you eat enough calories.

## c. The FST-7 Program

The name of this program stands for Fascial Stretch Training because the main goal of the program is to stretch the connective tissue surrounding your muscles (the fascia tissue) to speed muscle growth. To follow this program you would break up your routine into different muscle groups and perform 7 sets of 15 repetitions for the last exercise in each muscle group – you also need to limit your rest between sets to about 30 seconds. The main benefit of this program is its flexibility – it allows you to focus on certain muscle groups if you want to. The downside is that it may require longer recovery than other programs so you might not be able to work out as often.

### d. Upper/Lower Split Training

This type of training program involves splitting your training between the muscles in your upper body and those in your lower body. You typically work out two days in a row then take one day off – this schedule will allow you to hit each of the major muscle groups twice a week. For example, one day you would focus on leg exercises and the next on chest exercises. After a day off, you would work on your legs and back one day then chest and biceps the next. You can create your own program using a combination of isolation and compound exercises for each muscle group and, depending on the number of sets and repetitions, you can focus on either size or strength.

### e. Full Body Workout Program

This type of program is exactly what it sounds like – you work out your whole body by engaging all of the major muscle groups during each session. A full body workout program is a great choice for the beginner as long as you use a lower number of sets and repetitions but it can be challenging for an experienced bodybuilder if you use a higher frequency. This program is great for total body fitness but if you want to specialize in a specific body part you may need to add some isolation exercises.

# Chapter One: What is Bodybuilding?

# Chapter Two: The Three Core Principles

There are a variety of different bodybuilding programs out there and the program you choose will depend on what your goals are. For any bodybuilding program, however, the three core principles are the same: smart training, quality nutrition, and adequate rest. In this chapter you will learn some basic tips about how to train your body correctly as well as information about fueling your body properly with quality nutrition You will also receive some valuable information about incorporating recovery periods into your program to maximize your gains.

# Chapter Two: The Three Core Principles

## 1. Smart Training

Many bodybuilders will tell you that bodybuilding isn't so much about training hard as it is training smart. You can spend hours in the gym every day of the week but you won't see any real progress unless you are training correctly. Before getting into the basics about smart training, you should familiarize yourself with the process of muscle growth. If you do not already know and understand this process, you may be surprised to learn how muscle growth actually works – it is not simply a matter of your muscles increasing in size.

### a. The Process of Muscle Growth

Your body contains several different types of muscles – visceral muscle, cardiac muscle, and skeletal muscle. Visceral muscle is the kind of muscle found in your organs and blood vessels. This type of muscle is the weakest of all your muscles and it is controlled by the unconscious part of your mind – this is why it is sometimes called "involuntary muscle". Cardiac muscle is only found in the heart and its job is to pump blood throughout your body. This type of muscle is also involuntary – you cannot consciously control this type of muscle the way you can the muscles in your arms or legs, for example.

## Chapter Two: The Three Core Principles

The only voluntary muscle in your body is your skeletal muscles – these are the muscles that contract to move certain parts of your body according to your will. There are 650 different skeletal muscles in the body and they are all controlled by signals they receive from your motor neurons. When you activate your skeletal muscles you call them to contract and the more you do that, the greater control you have over your muscles and the stronger they get.

When it comes to the growth of your skeletal muscles, there are two different kinds of growth – hypertrophy and hyperplasia. Hypertrophy is also divided into two categories: sarcomere hypertrophy and sarcoplasmic hypertrophy. Sarcomere hypertrophy occurs when the contracting parts of your muscles, the sarcomeres, increase in size. Sarcoplasmic hypertrophy is the result of an increase in the non-contracting portion of your muscles. Hyperplasia, on the other hand, involves the increase in the number of muscle fibers, not the size.

As you work out, your muscles develop tiny tears in the muscle fibers. After the workout, your body repairs or replaces those damaged muscle fibers, often by fusing muscle fibers together to form a new strand – this is how sarcomere hypertrophy occurs. Of course, the only way to create the kind of muscle damage that leads to growth is to lift progressively heavier weights. Your body adapts to

# Chapter Two: The Three Core Principles

certain exercises the more you do them, so if you keep lifting the same amount of weight, you will maintain your current level of muscle and strength. That is where smart training comes into play.

### b. Tips for Training Correctly

Now that you understand the process of muscle growth you may be wondering what the best way to achieve it is. According to Bodybuilding.com, the goal of lifting weights is to encourage adaptation – you want your body to respond to the physical stress of lifting weights by increasing the size and number of your muscle fibers in order to adapt to the type of work you are doing. Then, once your body adapts to that level of performance, you increase the amount of physical stress by increasing the amount of weight and/or the number of sets and repetitions to encourage your body to adapt to the new level.

It is important to realize that hormones play a major role in muscle growth and repair. Testosterone is the main hormone associated with muscle growth because it helps to increase protein synthesis and to minimize protein breakdown. Unfortunately, most of the testosterone in the body is bound and unavailable for use. The best way to make that testosterone available is through strength training. When you work your muscles, testosterone helps

## Chapter Two: The Three Core Principles

to stimulate a response in your growth hormones, causing more neurotransmitters to gather at the site of the damaged muscle fibers to activate tissue growth.

If you were to ask a bodybuilder for advice on how to start lifting weights, he would probably tell you make sure that you work each major muscle group in your body once a week. This is the most basic principle of strength training and it is a simple enough concept for beginners to understand. The main muscle groups you want to work are your chest, back, shoulders, legs, and arms. Some bodybuilders divide these muscle groups down further, breaking the legs category into quadriceps and hamstrings as well as the arms category into biceps and triceps.

If the goal is to work each of these muscle groups once per week, there are different ways to go about doing that. If you refer back to the previous chapter, you will remember that some of the workout programs involved isolated muscle group exercises while others were built around compound exercises, working multiple muscle groups at a time. You can customize your workout plan depending on how many days you want to work out each week and which muscle groups you want to target. In order to maximize your gains, of course, you will also need to optimize your nutrition and your recovery.

## Chapter Two: The Three Core Principles

## *2. Quality Nutrition*

Nutrition for bodybuilding is very similar to the business concept of supply and demand – in order to fuel muscle growth and repair, your body demands a supply of certain nutrients. Similar to the concept of adaptation discussed in the last section, you can work out five days a week for two hours a day but unless you offer your body the right nutrition, you will not see any gains. Quality nutrition for bodybuilding is all about meeting the right macronutrient ratios.

Macronutrients are the nutrients that provide energy in the form of calories – this includes protein, fat, and

## Chapter Two: The Three Core Principles

carbohydrate. Vitamins and minerals are considered micronutrients – they are necessary for balanced nutrition but they do not contain any calories. Protein provides your body with 4 calories of energy per gram, which is the same as carbohydrate. Fat, on the other hand, provides 9 calories per gram which makes it a more highly concentrated source of energy.

Your body needs protein to sustain muscle growth and tissue repair – it also plays a role in immune function and hormone balance. Plus, you need plenty of protein in your diet to preserve your lean muscle mass. Fat gets a bad rap for causing weight gain, but it plays an important role in nutrition for bodybuilding. Fat is the most highly concentrated form of energy, plus it is necessary for absorbing certain vitamins. Carbohydrate is a less highly concentrated form of energy than fat, but it is more readily available and easier for the body to breakdown for immediate use.

The required amount of each macronutrient your body needs depends on a variety of factors. <u>To sustain muscle growth and repair, however, you should follow the nutrition tips below</u>:

- Try to consume 1 gram of protein per pound of bodyweight every day (Ex: a 150-pound man should consume at least 150g of protein daily).

- If you are new to bodybuilding, you may even want to increase it to 1.5g per pound of bodyweight for the first six months since this is when your muscles will respond the most to your training.

- Choose lean sources of protein like chicken, turkey, fish, and eggs to meet your protein needs.

- Try to consume 2 to 3 grams of carbohydrate per pound of bodyweight per day to provide fuel for your workouts.

- Choose slow-digesting carbohydrates like whole grains, beans, sweet potatoes, fruits and vegetables over simple carbohydrates like refined flour and sugary foods.

- Aim for about 20% to 30% of your daily calorie intake to come from healthy fats and try to get a balance of saturated and unsaturated fats.

- Choose red meat for protein and saturated fats plus avocado, olive oil, and nuts for unsaturated fats.

## Chapter Two: The Three Core Principles

- Try to get a balance of omega-3 and omega-6 fatty acids as well by eating fatty fish and nuts.

- In order to maximize muscle growth, try to consume about 20 calories per pound of bodyweight per day while maintaining the macronutrient ratios already mentioned.

If you follow the nutrition tips above, you will find yourself getting about 20% to 30% of your calories from protein, 40% to 60% from carbohydrate, and 20% to 30% from fat. To maintain these ratios you should aim to include protein and carbohydrate in every meal and try to eat every two to three hours to ensure that a steady supply of energy is available to maintain muscle growth all day long – this is the secret to staying lean. You should aim for six to eight meals per day and the size of these meals will be determined by your bodyweight. A 180-pound man, for example, would aim for 500 to 600 calories per meal in order to meet the 20 calorie per pound of bodyweight recommendation for daily calorie intake.

## 3. Adequate Rest

The third core principle of bodybuilding is rest. You already know the basics about how muscle growth works – your muscles grow when your body repairs the damage to your muscle fibers. This repair only occurs, however, during periods of rest. If you work out every day and do not give your muscles time to rest and recover, you may not see the gains you want. For this reason, sleep is an important part of any bodybuilding routine because this is when your body heals and recovers from the work you do during the day.

<u>To help you understand the importance of adequate rest for bodybuilding, consider the consequences of inadequate rest on the body</u>:

- Decreased energy levels
- Decreased testosterone levels
- Decreased growth hormone levels
- Increased catabolic hormones

If you don't give your body time to rest, you won't have the energy to get through your next workout and your testosterone levels won't be high enough to fuel hypertrophic muscle growth. An added consequence of inadequate rest is the increase of catabolic hormones – those are the hormones that break down muscle tissue. If you don't get enough rest between workouts you are putting yourself at risk for overtraining and this could increase your risk for injury, not to mention reduce your gains or stop them altogether.

The amount of rest you need between workouts may vary depending on the type of program you are following. General strength training recommendations call for one day of rest between workout days. This means that if you want to work out three days a week you might schedule your sessions for Monday, Wednesday and Friday.

<u>In order to maximize the efficacy of your rest periods, follow the recovery tips below:</u>

- Try to get at least 8 hours of sleep each night, even on the days you work out.

- On rest days, avoid activities that will increase your adrenaline levels, especially before bed.

- Avoid physical activity close to your bed time on workout days because an elevated heartrate will make it harder to fall asleep.

## Chapter Two: The Three Core Principles

- Avoid eating large meals right before bed and, if you do eat, focus on protein because it will be easier for your body to digest so more energy can be put toward muscle repair.

- Try to follow a consistent sleep schedule – this will help improve the quality of your sleep and maximize your recovery.

By following the three core principles of bodybuilding you can create your own individualized bodybuilding program to achieve the maximum result. In the next chapter you will receive specific information for bulking and cutting, two other principles that are very important for bodybuilders.

# Chapter Three: Bulking and Cutting

The main goal of bodybuilding is typically to build muscle, but there is also an aspect of weight loss involved – these processes are referred to as "bulking" and "cutting". In this chapter you will learn the basics about both of these concepts including common mistakes people make as well as tips for doing it right. You will also receive instruction for calculating your calorie needs so you can adjust your intake to maximize muscle gain or fat loss according to your individual goals.

## Chapter Three: Bulking and Cutting

## *1. When to Bulk and When to Cut*

Before you can learn about the appropriate times to bulk and cut, you first need to learn what bulking and cutting area. Bulking is simply the process of increasing calorie intake in order to gain weight and/or build muscle. Cutting is the process of reducing calorie intake with the goal of losing weight (particularly fat) to get leaner. Many professional bodybuilders go through cycles of bulking and cutting to prepare themselves for competition. Even if you are a beginner bodybuilder, you can use these principles to sculpt your own body.

Now that you know what bulking and cutting are, you may be curious to know how they work. Before getting into the proper methods for bulking and cutting, however, you might benefit from learning about some of the most common mistakes people make when bulking or cutting. <u>Some of the biggest mistakes people make when bulking include the following</u>:

- Increasing calorie intake without monitoring the actual amount of increase.
- Failure to monitor macronutrient ratios.
- Eating too much high-calorie junk food.
- Failure to do any cardiovascular activity.

## Chapter Three: Bulking and Cutting

- Focus on gaining weight quickly – usually leads to gaining fat, not muscle.

To some degree, simply increasing your calorie intake will lead to bulking. If you want to control your bulk and make sure that most of your gains are from muscle rather than fat, however, you need to be intentional about what and how much you are eating. Macronutrient ratios for bulking are different than they are for maintenance or cutting, so you need to learn how to bulk properly if you are going to do it right. <u>Below you will find some tips for bulking correctly</u>:

- Calculate your calorie intake to maximize muscle gain while minimizing fat gains.

- Aim for a daily calorie surplus around 250 calories for men and 125 for women (this surplus will be calculated based on your daily calorie maintenance level).

- Aim for a rate of weight gain around 0.5 pounds per week for men and 0.25 pounds per week for women.

- Focus on your macronutrient ratios and optimize them to achieve your goals.

## Chapter Three: Bulking and Cutting

The macronutrient ratio you choose to follow will vary according to your goals. Keep in mind that you can either emphasize muscle gain OR fat loss – you cannot achieve your maximum potential for both of these things simultaneously. Why? Because gaining muscle requires a surplus of calories while losing fat requires a deficit. The key to bulking properly is the find the right balance of calories and macronutrients to gain muscle mass while minimizing fat gain. Once you have achieved your goal for muscle gain you can then cut to shed excess fat.

As is true for bulking, there is a right way and a wrong way to go about cutting. <u>Below you will find a list of common mistakes people make when cutting</u>:

- Making significant reductions in daily calorie intake.
- Increasing cardiovascular activity too much.
- Lifting lower weight at higher reps (switching from high weight and low reps).
- Switching from eating mainly junk food to eating only "clean" foods.
- Becoming too focused on nutrient intake.

You are probably already familiar with the basic principle behind cutting – fewer calories means more weight loss. But you need to be very careful about how much you reduce your calorie intake or else you might end up losing some of the muscle you just worked so hard to

## Chapter Three: Bulking and Cutting

build. Like bulking, cutting requires a delicate balance of calorie intake and macronutrient ratios. <u>Below you will find some tips for cutting correctly</u>:

- Aim for slow weight loss rather than fast weight loss – it will be easier to maintain and less likely to come from muscle loss than fat loss.

- Calculate your calorie needs for maintenance and create a moderate deficit, about 20% less than your calorie maintenance level.

- Make an effort to maintain your macronutrient ratios during cutting to preserve lean muscle mass.

- Still aim for 1 to 1.5g of protein per pound of bodyweight in order to maintain muscle mass while losing fat.

Now that you understand the basics about bulking and cutting you may be eager to apply these principles. In the next section you will learn how to calculate your own calorie needs so you can adjust them for bulking and for cutting according to your goals.

## 2. Calculating Calorie Intake

In order to determine how many calories you need to consume to bulk or to cut, you first need to calculate your calorie maintenance level – this is simply the number of calories you can consume to maintain your current weight and body composition. <u>Remember, your calorie maintenance level will vary depending on a number of important factors including</u>:

- Age
- Gender
- Height
- Weight
- Activity level
- Metabolic rate

# Chapter Three: Bulking and Cutting

## a. Calculating Calorie Maintenance Level

There are several different formulas you can use to calculate your calorie needs. The simplest method (though it does leave a large margin of error) is as follows:

**Body Weight (in lbs.) x 14-17 (pick a number)**

To use this formula, you simply measure your current bodyweight in pounds and then multiply it by 14. Then, multiply your bodyweight by 17. Somewhere in between those two numbers is your ideal calorie maintenance level. For example, a 180-pound man would have a calorie maintenance level somewhere between 2,520 and 3,060 calories per day. People who are older or less active should stick to the lower end of this calorie spectrum while younger and more active individuals should stick to the higher end. Also, women are likely to have lower calorie maintenance levels than men.

If you want a little more accuracy in terms of calculating your calorie maintenance level, you can try using the Mifflin-St. Jeor Equation which is shown below. This equation will give you a baseline for calorie intake which you can then customize according to your activity level. <u>You can find free calculators using the Mifflin-St. Jeor</u>

## Chapter Three: Bulking and Cutting

Equation online but the basic formula is as follows:

**Men**: [10 x (weight in kg)] + [6.25 x (height in cm)] – [5 x age] + 5

**Women**: [10x(weight in kg)] + [6.25x(height cm)] – [5x age] -161

This is the formula that the American Dietetic Association (ADA) has deemed to be the most accurate. If you are a beginner bodybuilder, this is probably the formula you want to use. If you are an experienced bodybuilder and already have a lot of lean muscle mass (especially if you know exactly what percentage), you can try the Katch-McArdle formula instead. This formula is shown below – fat free mass is calculated by multiplying weight by body fat percentage and subtracting that value from total body weight.

**Calorie Intake = 21.6 x (fat free mass) + 370**

Using the Mifflin-St. Jeor Equation, a 180-pound man who is 30 years old and 6-feet tall would have a calorie maintenance level of 2,149 if he were completely sedentary. His calorie needs would increase in proportion to his activity level. If he were lightly active, his calorie intake would be about 2,463 but if he were highly active it would

# Chapter Three: Bulking and Cutting

increase to 3,045. Again, if you choose to use this formula to calculate your own calorie maintenance level, your best bet is to find a free calculator online so you can input your activity level for the greatest accuracy.

### b. Calculating Bulking Calorie Level

Now that you know how many calories you can consume on a daily basis to maintain your current weight you can use that number to determine how many calories you should be consuming to gain muscle. Remember, the goal is to gain as much lean muscle mass as possible while minimizing fat gain. To do this, you should only increase your calorie intake by about 250 calories for men or by 125 calories for women. Using the example of the lightly active 180-pound man from the last section, he would be consuming about 2,713 calories daily – if he were highly active, this would increase to 3,295.

### c. Calculating Cutting Calorie Level

Calculating calorie intake for cutting is not exactly the opposite of calculating calories for bulking – you do not subtract a specific number from your daily intake. Rather, you need to calculate a percentage of your daily intake to determine your calorie level for cutting. The best percentage to go with is 20%. Using the example from the last section, a 20% reduction in calorie intake for a lightly active 180-pound man would have a deficit of about 493 calories – that leaves him with a total of about 1,970 calories. The same man would have a deficit of about 609 calories if he were highly active, leaving a total of 2,436 calories daily.

## 3. *Macronutrient Ratios*

Now that you understand the concepts of bulking and cutting and you have calculated your calorie maintenance level you are ready to get into the details of macronutrient ratios for cutting and bulking. Remember, bulking requires a slight calorie surplus but you still want to monitor your macronutrient ratios to make sure you are gaining muscle, not fat. When cutting, your macronutrient ratios are still just as important because you want to maximize fat loss while maintaining muscle mass.

The ideal macronutrient ratio for bulking is 40% to 60% carbohydrate, 25% to 35% protein, and 15% to 25% fat. Focusing on carbohydrates for bulking will ensure that your body has the energy you need to fuel your workouts so you can maximize your gains. Moderate protein levels will ensure proper muscle repair while moderate fat levels ensure proper energy stores.

The ideal macronutrient ratio for cutting is 10% to 30% carbohydrate, 40% to 50% protein and 30% to 40% fat. You still need some carbohydrate for immediate energy, but more of your energy will come from fat. Increasing your fat consumption encourages your body to start burning fat for fuel – especially since there are fewer carbohydrates available. Increasing your protein levels will also help to make sure you maintain lean muscle mass while burning excess fat.

You have probably noticed that the macronutrient ratios provided for bulking and cutting are given in a range of values rather than a hard-fast number. This is because the macronutrient ratio that is ideal for you will vary depending on several factors including your body type. There are three main body types – ectomorph, mesomorph, and endomorph. <u>You will find a brief overview of each body type below</u>:

- **Ectomorph** – This body type is naturally slender with delicate bone structure and a fast metabolism. People with this body type often find it easy to put on weight and mass. Ectomorphs should stick to the higher end of the carb ratio to gain mass and the lower end to lose fat.

- **Mesomorph** – This body type tends to be more muscular with an athletic build, defined muscle, and a dense bone structure. People with this body type have trouble gaining muscle or losing fat. Mesomorphs should stick to the middle range for carbohydrates.

- **Endomorph** – This body type tends to be a little soft, having a round or pear-shaped body with a stocky build and slower metabolism. People with this body type can but on a lot of muscle but they are also more likely to store fat. Endomorphs should stick to the lower end of the carbohydrate range.

In addition to considering your body type you may also need to think about things such as your age, gender, and activity level. Finding the right balance of calories and macronutrients can take some time, so keep a close watch on your weight and body composition as you go. Your body will tell you whether you need to increase or decrease your calorie intake a little bit more and you can play around with macronutrient ratios until you find the one that works best for you and your body.

# Chapter Three: Bulking and Cutting

# Chapter Four: Nutrition for Bodybuilding

By now you should have a basic understanding of what bodybuilding and how it works. Lifting weights plays a major role in helping you to sculpt your body, but all of your work will not pay off unless you fuel your body correctly. In this chapter you will learn the basics about nutrition for bodybuilding including tips to burn fat and build muscle as well as nutrition myths and mistakes that you should try to avoid. This chapter will help you to develop your own diet in a way that you will be able to maximize your bodybuilding results.

## Chapter Four: Nutrition for Bodybuilding

### 1. *Diet Tips to Burn Fat*

As you have already learned, bodybuilders often go back and forth between periods of bulking and cutting. During cutting periods, it is essential that you customize your diet plan to maximize your fat-burning results. <u>Below you will find a collection of tips to help you burn more fat</u>:

- Don't go off the deep end with a low-calorie diet – you need to eat enough to maintain lean muscle mass while burning fat, so keep your calorie deficit moderate.

- Reduce your carbohydrate intake, focusing more on protein and fat (healthy fats) – the carbs you do eat should come from whole grains, beans, and vegetables instead of starchy or sugary foods.

- Try to keep eating six to eight small meals throughout the day so your body is constantly burning calories and so you don't get too hungry.

- Consider adding a fat-burner to your diet – the most effective fat-burners are made with ECA (ephedrine,

## Chapter Four: Nutrition for Bodybuilding

caffeine, and aspirin).

- Pay special attention to your post-workout meal to prevent muscle loss – a protein shake that contains both casein and whey protein is a good option.

- Build your diet around less calorie-dense foods – this will allow you to eat more so that you feel full while still maintaining your calorie deficit.

- Drink plenty of water throughout the day – drinking a lot of water will help to reduce water retention and you won't be as hungry.

- Don't make the mistake of avoiding fats while you are cutting – fats from clean oils, nuts and seeds are an essential part of a bodybuilder's diet no matter what.

- Add a little extra cardio to your routine but do not overdo it – if you add too much cardio you could end up burning through muscle instead of fat.

- Make sure you get plenty of sleep so your body has time to recover and repair – this is especially important if you're adding more cardio to your routine.

By following the tips above you should have no trouble cutting fat. The key is to give yourself plenty of time to lose the extra fat and to maintain a healthy diet while you do so. If you want to set a deadline for your weight loss, give yourself about 2 months for every 10 pounds you hope to lose with an extra week or two tacked on for good measure, just in case you run into obstacles.

## 2. Nutrition Tips for Building Muscle

Simply increasing your daily calorie intake may not be enough to build muscle – you need to be intentional about what kind of foods you are eating to make sure you are gaining muscle, not fat. It is a delicate line to walk, but you will get the hang of it with adequate time and practice. <u>Below you will find a collection of nutrition tips to help you build muscle</u>:

- Focus on lean protein options like chicken, turkey, eggs, fish, and dairy – these are also complete

## Chapter Four: Nutrition for Bodybuilding

sources of protein.

- Don't cut your carbohydrate intake too low – you need about 2 to 3 grams per pound of bodyweight to keep your glycogen stores full and to provide fuel for your workouts.

- Eat plenty of healthy fats to maintain testosterone levels and for concentrated energy – aim for 20% to 30% of your daily consumption from fats.

- Maintain a positive calorie balance throughout the day – that means eating more calories than you burn and keeping your body fueled throughout the day.

- Eat a small meal every two to three hours – each meal should contain lean protein and digestible carbs to supply energy and amino acids for continuous muscle growth.

- Make sure to get at least 20 grams of protein and 40 grams of slow-digesting carbs both before each workout – protein shakes are a great way to accomplish this.

## Chapter Four: Nutrition for Bodybuilding

- Make sure you get about 3 to 5 grams of creatine in your pre- and post-workout meals or shakes – you can buy creatine powder and add it directly.

- Refuel with 20 to 40 grams of protein and 60 to 100 grams of fast-digesting carbs after each workout – some options include white bread, baked potato, and sports drinks.

- Have a protein-rich snack before bed – some great options include cottage cheese, mixed nuts, and peanut butter.

- Take HMB (β-Hydroxy β-methylbutyric acid) supplements with your first meal of the day and both before and after your workouts – you may also want to take another one before bed to prevent muscle breakdown.

By following the tips above you can maximize your muscle gains without gaining too much fat. Growing muscle is about providing your body with the protein it needs to build new muscle while also providing it with the fuel it needs to sustain you through your workouts.

## Chapter Four: Nutrition for Bodybuilding

## *3. Nutrition Myths and Mistakes to Avoid*

Now that you've received some tips for shedding fat and building muscle you may feel as though you know everything you need to know about nutrition for bodybuilding. Many beginner bodybuilders still fall prey to certain myths and misconceptions, however, even after learning the basics for bulking and cutting. To save yourself some time and hassle, consider the following myths and mistakes so you do not make them yourself:

**Myth**: *You can only eat "clean" foods.*

It makes sense that if you want to build a better body you need to improve your nutrition, but it is easy to get too strict in terms of your diet, especially while cutting. If you restrict your diet too severely you put yourself at risk for cravings and you are more likely to give in to temptation in a big way. Rather, aim to eat clean about 90% of the time and give yourself 10% wiggle room.

**Myth**: *You can't eat fat while you're cutting.*

Many people mistakenly assume that in order to shed body fat you must completely remove fat from your diet. In reality, increasing your fat consumption (while still maintaining a calorie deficit) can actually help you to burn MORE fat. Just make sure that most of the fat you consume comes from monounsaturated fats like avocado, olive oil, nuts and seeds – some saturated fats from beef and other red meats are also okay.

**Myth**: *Carbs are carbs, it doesn't matter what kind.*

To some degree, carbohydrates provide your body with a fast source of energy no matter what kind of carbohydrate it is. There are, however, times when certain kinds of carbs are better than others. Before a workout, for example, you want to focus on slow-digesting carbs like whole grains so you will have enough energy to last throughout your routine. After a workout you want to refill the glycogen stores in your muscles as quickly as possible so you don't lose muscle – that is when you want to fast-digesting carbs like white bread and potatoes.

**Myth**: *The more you eat, the more you gain.*

If you operate at a calorie surplus you will gain – but it won't all be muscle. Your body is capable of gaining weight very quickly, but its ability to put on new muscle is limited.

## Chapter Four: Nutrition for Bodybuilding

If you eat more calories than your body can use, the extra will be stored as fat. If you want to gain muscle you really only need to be operating at a calorie surplus of 250 calories for men and 125 calories for women. More important is the macronutrient ratio you follow – you need plenty of carbohydrate and protein to maximize muscle growth.

**Myth**: *Eggs are bad because they're high in cholesterol.*

You have probably heard that eggs are bad because they are high in cholesterol. But do not go out and buy cartons of egg whites just yet. It is true that eggs contain about 450mg of cholesterol (your daily recommended dose is 300mg), but the kind of cholesterol found in eggs is dietary cholesterol – it is different from the kind of cholesterol that clogs your arteries. If you are worried about cholesterol you can eat a mixture of whole eggs and egg whites.

**Myth**: *Going gluten-free is an easy way to lose weight.*

If you pay attention to the latest fads that hit the health and diet industry you've probably heard a lot of bad things about gluten. While it is true that gluten can be very bad for people with Celiac disease or gluten intolerance, it is completely fine for most people. Cutting gluten out of your diet isn't a magical weight loss solution – you still have to operate at a calorie deficit to lose weight. The truth is that many gluten-free packaged foods are just as high in sugar, fat, and calories as the regular versions.

**Myth**: *Detoxing is a great way to start my cut.*

Countless people have jumped onto the detox bandwagon lately, especially people who are trying to lose weight. Some detoxes might be beneficial in terms of increasing your intake of antioxidants, vitamins, and minerals, but most of them are dangerously low in calories and protein. While detoxing you might think that you are ridding your body of accumulated toxins, but you may actually be burning through muscle and slowing down your metabolism.

# Chapter Four: Nutrition for Bodybuilding

# Chapter Five: What to Eat and When

Now that you have an understanding of nutrition for bodybuilding in general you are ready to learn the details about pre-workout and post-workout nutrition. The food you eat before, during and after a workout can have a serious impact on your performance as well as your progress. In this chapter you will receive tips for fueling your body properly in preparation for a workout as well as tips for keeping your body going during a hard workout. You will also receive helpful information about refeeding after a workout to maximize your recovery as well as your muscle gains.

## Chapter Five: What to Eat and When

## 1. Pre-Workout Nutrition

The food you eat before you work out is incredibly important because it will provide your body with the fuel you need to achieve the maximum results. The goal of pre-workout nutrition is to prepare your body to perform at its highest level by providing it with slow-burning energy. Your pre-workout meal should consist of at least 20 to 40 grams of protein and at least 40 and 80 grams of carbohydrate within about 30 minutes of starting your workout. For a more exact calculation, aim for about 0.25g of protein per pound of body weight and 0.25g of carbohydrates per pound of body weight. It is best to consume this in some form of pre-workout drink so your body will be able to digest it quickly for energy.

In addition to fueling your body 30 minutes before your workout you should also have a balanced meal about 1 ½ to 2 hours before your workout. This meal should contain both protein and carbohydrates but it should be low in fat. In terms of what kind of carbohydrates you should be consuming, your pre-workout meal should consist primarily of slow-digesting carbs like whole grains. Don't forget about protein either! Your pre-workout meal should contain some lean protein from things like white fish, chicken breast, and egg whites.

## 2. During Workout Nutrition

During your workout you want to keep your body hydrated and you want to provide your muscles with protein to fuel repair and recovery. You should aim for consuming between 20 and 40 grams of protein during your workout, especially if your workout is going to be a long one. If you are working out for 30 minutes or less, however, you can wait until after you finish to refuel.

You have two main options for nutrition during a workout – bars or drinks. Drinks are usually the more convenient option and they can be absorbed by your body faster than bars. Many bodybuilders mix whey protein powder with water in a shaker bottle to drink during their workouts. You can also purchase Ready-to-Drink (RTD) protein beverages to drink during your workout.

## 3. Post-Workout Nutrition

After working out you will need to replenish your body's stores of glycogen so your body doesn't start burning muscle for fuel. What you put into your body immediately after you work out will also have a direct impact on your soreness and recovery. Like your pre-workout meal, your post-workout meal should consist primarily of carbohydrates and protein. Aim for at least 20 to 40 grams of protein and at least 60 to 100 grams of carbohydrate. For a more exact calculation, shoot for 0.25g of protein per pound bodyweight and 0.25 to 0.5g of carbohydrate per pound of bodyweight.

The easiest way to achieve these macros post-workout is to drink a post-workout drink. If you want something a little more satisfying than a post-workout drink, eat some fast-digesting carbs like white bread or potatoes in addition to some chicken breast or another form of lean protein. You can also combine the two, using a whey protein shake for your protein and some kind of high-glycemic carbohydrate for your carbs.

# Chapter Five: What to Eat and When

# Chapter Six: Fat-Burning Recipes for Cutting

When you are trying to lose fat, you need to do more than just cut calories. In fact, a moderate reduction in calorie intake is only half of the equation – you also need to be mindful about what you eat. The best recipes for fat-burning are made with lean protein, healthy fats, and low in carbohydrates. In this chapter you will receive a collection of breakfast recipes, snacks and smoothies, and main entrees for cutting.

## Chapter Six: Fat-Burning Recipes for Cutting

## 1. Breakfast Recipes

### Recipes Included in this Section:

Tomato Basil Egg White Omelet

Cinnamon Steel-Cut Oats

Spinach and Mushroom Frittata

Cottage Cheese Breakfast Parfait

Sautéed Sweet Potato Hash

Herbed Spinach Egg White Omelet

Yogurt and Fresh Berry Parfait

# Chapter Six: Fat-Burning Recipes for Cutting

## Tomato Basil Egg White Omelet

**Servings**: 1

**Ingredients**:

- 1 teaspoon olive oil, divided
- 1 small vine-ripened tomato, cored and chopped
- 2 tablespoons diced yellow onion
- 1 clove minced garlic
- 4 large egg whites, beaten
- 1 tablespoon fresh chopped chives
- Salt and pepper to taste
- 1 to 2 tablespoons fresh chopped basil

**Instructions**:

1. Heat ½ teaspoon olive oil in a small skillet over medium heat.
2. Add the tomato, onion and garlic then cook for 4 to 5 minutes until tender.
3. Spoon the vegetables into a bowl then reheat the skillet with the remaining oil.
4. Whisk together the egg whites, chives, salt and pepper in a small bowl.
5. Pour the mixture into the skillet and cook for 1 minute without disturbing.
6. Continue to cook the egg whites until almost set then spoon the vegetable mixture over half the omelet.
7. Sprinkle on the basil then fold the uncooked half of the omelet over the filling.
8. Cook for 30 to 60 seconds or until the egg is set.

## Chapter Six: Fat-Burning Recipes for Cutting

### Cinnamon Steel-Cut Oats

**Servings**: 4 to 6

**Ingredients**:

- 3 ½ cups water
- 1 cup steel-cut oats, uncooked
- Pinch salt
- 1 ½ teaspoons vanilla extract
- 1 teaspoon ground cinnamon

**Instructions**:

1. Bring the water to boil in a small saucepan.
2. Stir in the oats and salt then bring to a boil again.
3. Reduce heat and simmer, covered, for 20 to 30 minutes until thick and creamy.
4. Remove from heat then stir in the vanilla and cinnamon.
5. Spoon into bowls and serve hot.

## Spinach and Mushroom Frittata

**Servings**: 1

**Ingredients**:

- 4 crimini mushrooms, sliced thin
- 1 cup fresh chopped spinach
- 1 cup liquid egg whites
- Salt and pepper to taste

**Instructions**:

1. Preheat the broiler in your oven to high heat.
2. Grease a small skillet with cooking spray.
3. Add the mushrooms and cook for 3 minutes until they start to sweat.
4. Stir in the spinach and cook for 2 minutes until wilted.
5. Beat the egg whites until frothy then whisk in the salt and pepper.
6. Pour the mixture into the skillet and allow to cook for 2 minutes.
7. Lift the edges of the cooked egg, allowing the uncooked egg to spread underneath.
8. Transfer the skillet to the oven and broil for 2 to 3 minutes until the eggs are puffed.

## Cottage Cheese Breakfast Parfait

**Servings**: 2

**Ingredients**:

- 1 ½ to 2 cups low-fat cottage cheese
- 2 medium ripe bananas, peeled and sliced
- 2 tablespoons ground flaxseed
- Pinch ground cinnamon

**Instructions**:

1. Spoon the cottage cheese into two parfait glasses, dividing it evenly.
2. Spoon the sliced banana over the cottage cheese.
3. Sprinkle with ground flaxseed and cinnamon then serve immediately.

## Chapter Six: Fat-Burning Recipes for Cutting

### Sautéed Sweet Potato Hash

**Servings**: 4 to 6

**Ingredients**:

- 3 medium sweet potatoes, peeled and halved
- ½ small yellow onion, chopped
- 1 medium carrot, peeled and diced
- ½ small red pepper, cored and diced
- 1 clove minced garlic
- 1 teaspoon ground cumin
- ½ teaspoon chili powder
- Salt and pepper to taste
- 2 tablespoons fresh chopped parsley

**Instructions**:

1. Bring a pot of salted water to boil then add the sweet potatoes.
2. Simmer the sweet potatoes until tender then drain and pat dry.
3. Grease a medium skillet with cooking spray and heat it over medium heat.
4. Dice the sweet potatoes and add them to the skillet.
5. Stir in the onions, carrot, red pepper and garlic.
6. Season with cumin, chili powder, salt and pepper.
7. Sauté for 5 to 6 minutes until the vegetables start to brown.
8. Stir in the parsley then cook for 1 minute undisturbed. Serve hot.

## Herbed Spinach Egg White Omelet

**Servings**: 1

**Ingredients**:

- 1 teaspoon olive oil, divided
- 1 cup fresh chopped spinach
- 1 clove minced garlic
- 4 large egg whites, beaten
- 2 tablespoons fresh chopped herbs
- Salt and pepper to taste

**Instructions**:

1. Heat ½ teaspoon olive oil in a small skillet over medium heat.
2. Add the spinach garlic then cook for 2 to 3 minutes until wilted.
3. Spoon the spinach into a bowl then reheat the skillet with the remaining oil.
4. Whisk together the egg whites, herbs, salt and pepper in a small bowl.
5. Pour the mixture into the skillet and cook for 1 minute without disturbing.
6. Continue to cook the egg whites until almost set then spoon the spinach mixture over half the omelet.
7. Fold the uncooked half of the omelet over the filling and cook for 30 to 60 seconds or until the egg is set.

## Chapter Six: Fat-Burning Recipes for Cutting

### Yogurt and Fresh Berry Parfait

**Servings**: 2

**Ingredients**:

- 1 ½ cups fat-free yogurt, plain
- ¼ to 1/3 cup whole-grain granola
- 1 cup fresh berries, your choice

**Instructions**:

1. Spoon ¼ cup yogurt into each of two parfait glasses.
2. Top the yogurt in each glass with 2 tablespoons of whole-grain granola and ¼ cup fresh berries.
3. Add another ½ cup of yogurt to each glass.
4. Top with the remaining granola and fresh berries to serve.

## Chapter Six: Fat-Burning Recipes for Cutting

### *2. Snacks and Green Smoothies*

**Recipes Included in this Section:**

Cottage Cheese Crackers with Smoked Salmon

Easy Green Tea Smoothie

Spinach Parmesan Snack Muffins

Banana Oatmeal Smoothie

Baked Oatmeal Muffins

Spinach Green Apple Smoothie

## Chapter Six: Fat-Burning Recipes for Cutting

## Cottage Cheese Crackers with Smoked Salmon

**Servings**: 1

**Ingredients**:

- 6 whole-grain crackers
- 6 tablespoons low-fat cottage cheese
- 1 medium Roma tomato, sliced thin
- 2 ounces smoked salmon, sliced thin
- Salt and pepper to taste

**Instructions**:

1. Place the crackers on a plate.
2. Spread the cottage cheese on the crackers.
3. Top each cracker with a slice of tomato.
4. Add a few slices of smoked salmon to each cracker and season with salt and pepper to taste.

# Chapter Six: Fat-Burning Recipes for Cutting

### Easy Green Tea Smoothie

**Servings**: 1

**Ingredients**:

- 1 ½ cups fresh chopped baby spinach
- 1 medium frozen banana, peeled and sliced
- 1 cup brewed green tea, cooled
- ½ cup fat-free yogurt, plain
- ½ cup ice cubes

**Instructions**:

1. Combine all of the ingredients in high-speed blender.
2. Pulse the mixture several times to chop the ingredients.
3. Blend on high-speed for 30 to 60 seconds until smooth.
4. Pour the smoothie into a glass and enjoy immediately.

## Spinach Parmesan Snack Muffins

**Servings**: 8

**Ingredients**:

- 12 ounces fresh chopped spinach
- 2 large eggs, beaten well
- ½ cup low-fat cottage cheese
- 1/3 cup grated reduced-fat parmesan cheese
- ½ teaspoon minced garlic
- Salt and pepper to taste

**Instructions**:

1. Preheat the oven to 400°F and grease a muffin pan with cooking spray.
2. Place the spinach in a food processor and pulse to chop.
3. Beat together the eggs, cottage cheese, parmesan cheese, and garlic in a mixing bowl.
4. Stir in the chopped spinach then season with salt and pepper to taste.
5. Spoon the mixture into 8 cups of the muffin pan.
6. Bake for 20 minutes or until the muffins are set.
7. Cool for 5 minutes in the pan then turn out onto a plate to serve.

# Chapter Six: Fat-Burning Recipes for Cutting

## Banana Oatmeal Smoothie

**Servings**: 1

**Ingredients**:

- 1 medium frozen banana, peeled and sliced
- ¾ cup fat-free milk
- ½ cup fat-free yogurt, plain
- ¼ cup old-fashioned oats
- ¼ teaspoon ground cinnamon

**Instructions**:

1. Combine all of the ingredients in high-speed blender.
2. Pulse the mixture several times to chop the ingredients.
3. Blend on high-speed for 30 to 60 seconds until smooth.
4. Pour the smoothie into a glass and enjoy immediately.

# Chapter Six: Fat-Burning Recipes for Cutting

## Baked Oatmeal Muffins

**Servings**: 12

**Ingredients**:

- 1 ½ cups old-fashioned oats
- ¼ cup raw sunflower seeds
- 2 ½ tablespoons chia seeds
- 1 teaspoon baking powder
- 1 teaspoon ground cinnamon
- ¼ teaspoon salt
- 2 tablespoons natural almond butter
- 1 large egg, beaten well
- ¾ cups fat-free milk

**Instructions**:

1. Preheat the oven to 350°F and grease a regular muffin pan with paper liners.
2. Stir together the oats, sunflower seeds, chia seeds, baking powder, cinnamon and salt in a mixing bowl.
3. In another bowl, beat together the almond butter and egg then slowly whisk in the milk.
4. Stir the wet ingredients into the dry ingredients.
5. Spoon the oatmeal mixture into the muffin pan then bake for 25 to 30 minutes until set.
6. Cool the muffins for 5 minutes then turn out onto a wire rack to cool completely.

## Spinach Green Apple Smoothie

**Servings**: 1

**Ingredients**:

- 2 cups fresh chopped baby spinach
- 1 medium green apple, peeled, cored and chopped
- 1 cup coconut water
- ½ cup ice cubes
- ½ cup fat-free yogurt, plain

**Instructions**:

1. Combine all of the ingredients in high-speed blender.
2. Pulse the mixture several times to chop the ingredients.
3. Blend on high-speed for 30 to 60 seconds until smooth.
4. Pour the smoothie into a glass and enjoy immediately.

## Chapter Six: Fat-Burning Recipes for Cutting

## 3. Entrée Recipes

**Recipes Included in this Section**:

Mediterranean-Style Tuna Salad

Almond-Crusted Baked Halibut

Creamy Carrot Ginger Soup

Slow Cooker Turkey Sloppy Joes

Balsamic Glazed Grilled Salmon

Spinach Salad with Green Apples

## Chapter Six: Fat-Burning Recipes for Cutting

### Mediterranean-Style Tuna Salad

**Servings**: 4

**Ingredients**:

- 2 (6-ounce) cans tuna in water, drained
- ¼ cup thinly sliced red onion
- 1/3 cup sliced black olives
- ¼ cup reduced fat feta cheese, crumbled
- ¼ cup fresh chopped parsley
- 2 tablespoons olive oil
- 1 tablespoon fresh lemon juice
- 1 tablespoon red wine vinegar
- Salt and pepper to taste
- Chopped lettuce

**Instructions**:

1. Flake the tuna into a mixing bowl.
2. Toss in the red onion, olives, feta cheese, and parsley.
3. Stir in the olive oil, lemon juice, red wine vinegar, salt and pepper.
4. Serve the tuna salad over chopped lettuce.

## Almond-Crusted Baked Halibut

**Servings**: 4

**Ingredients**:

- 4 (6-ounce) boneless halibut fillets
- Salt and pepper to taste
- ¼ cup whole-wheat breadcrumbs
- ¼ cup finely chopped almonds
- 1 teaspoon dried parsley
- 2 large egg whites
- 1 large lemon, cut into wedges

**Instructions**:

1. Preheat the oven to 350°F and line a baking sheet with parchment paper.
2. Rinse the fillets with water then pat dry and season with salt and pepper to taste.
3. Combine the breadcrumbs, almonds and parsley in a shallow dish.
4. Beat the egg whites in a separate dish.
5. Dip the fillets into the egg then dredge in the almond mixture.
6. Place the fillets on the baking sheet and bake for 12 to 15 minutes until the flesh flakes easily with a fork.
7. Serve the fillets hot with lemon wedges.

## Creamy Carrot Ginger Soup

**Servings**: 4 to 6

**Ingredients**:

- 1 tablespoon olive oil
- 2 lbs. fresh chopped carrots
- 2 large yellow onion, chopped
- Salt and pepper to taste
- 1 teaspoon fresh minced ginger
- 1 clove minced garlic
- 5 cups low-sodium chicken broth

**Instructions**:

1. Heat the oil in a large saucepan over medium heat.
2. Add the carrots and onions and cook for 6 to 8 minutes until the onions are tender.
3. Season with salt and pepper to taste.
4. Stir in the ginger and garlic then cook for 2 minutes.
5. Whisk in the chicken broth then bring to a simmer.
6. Cover and simmer on low heat for 20 minutes until the carrots are very tender.
7. Remove from heat and puree the soup using an immersion blender.
8. Adjust the seasonings to taste and serve hot.

# Chapter Six: Fat-Burning Recipes for Cutting

## Slow Cooker Turkey Sloppy Joes

**Servings**: 6 to 8

**Ingredients**:

- 1 teaspoon olive oil
- 1 lbs. lean ground turkey breast
- 1 medium yellow onion, chopped
- 1 stalk celery, diced
- ½ small red pepper, cored and diced
- 1 (10.5-ounce) can condensed tomato soup
- ½ cup tomato sauce
- 3 tablespoons Dijon mustard
- Salt and pepper to taste
- Whole-grain sandwich buns

**Instructions**:

1. Heat the oil in a large skillet over medium heat.
2. Add the turkey, onion, celery and red pepper.
3. Cook for 5 to 6 minutes until the turkey is browned then drain the fat.
4. Transfer the mixture to the slow cooker.
5. Stir in the canned soup, tomato sauce, and mustard.
6. Season with salt and pepper to taste then cover the slow cooker.
7. Cook on low heat for 4 hours then serve on whole-grain sandwich buns.

## Chapter Six: Fat-Burning Recipes for Cutting

**Balsamic Glazed Grilled Salmon**

**Servings**: 4

**Ingredients**:

- ¼ cup balsamic vinegar
- ¼ cup water
- 1 tablespoon fresh lemon juice
- 1 tablespoon honey
- 4 (6-ounce) boneless salmon fillets
- Salt and pepper to taste

**Instructions**:

1. Whisk together the balsamic vinegar, water, lemon juice and honey in a small saucepan.
2. Simmer the mixture on medium-low heat until reduced by half.
3. Rinse the salmon in cool water then pat dry and season with salt and pepper to taste.
4. Preheat the grill to medium-high heat and brush the grates with olive oil.
5. Place the fillets on the grill and cook for 4 to 5 minutes on each side until cooked through.
6. Serve the fillets hot drizzled with balsamic glaze.

## Spinach Salad with Green Apples

**Servings**: 4

**Ingredients**:

- 6 cups chopped green spinach
- 1 cup thinly sliced mushrooms
- ¼ cup thinly sliced red onion
- 2 tablespoons olive oil
- 1 ½ tablespoons apple cider vinegar
- 1 tablespoon fresh lemon juice
- 1 teaspoon Dijon mustard
- Salt and pepper to taste
- 1 large green apple, cored and sliced thin

**Instructions**:

1. Toss together the spinach, mushrooms and red onion in a salad bowl.
2. Whisk together the olive oil, vinegar, lemon juice and mustard in a small bowl.
3. Season with salt and pepper to taste then toss the dressing with the salad.
4. Divide the salad among four salad plates and top with sliced green apple to serve.

# Chapter Seven: Muscle-Building Recipes for Bulking

## 1. Breakfast Recipes

**Recipes Included in this Section**:

Eggs Baked in Avocado

Corned Beef Hash with Fried Eggs

Easy Spanish Omelet

Sausage and Egg Breakfast Casserole

Apple Cinnamon Breakfast Quinoa

Ham and Cheese Egg Muffins

# Chapter Seven: Muscle-Building Recipes for Bulking

## Eggs Baked in Avocado

**Servings**: 4

**Ingredients**:

- 2 large ripe avocadoes
- 4 large eggs
- Salt and pepper to taste
- ¼ cup shredded cheese

**Instructions**:

1. Preheat the oven to 425°F.
2. Cut the avocados in half and remove the pits.
3. Use a spoon to scoop out a few tablespoons of flesh from the middle of each half.
4. Place the avocado halves upright in a glass baking dish.
5. Crack one egg into the center of each avocado half and season with salt and pepper to taste.
6. Bake for 10 minutes then sprinkle with cheese and bake for another 5 to 10 minutes until the avocado is tender.

## Corned Beef Hash with Fried Eggs

**Servings**: 4

**Ingredients**:

- 1 lbs. Russet potatoes, peeled and diced
- 1 lbs. cooked corned beef, chopped
- 1 tablespoon olive oil
- 1 medium yellow onion, chopped
- Salt and pepper to taste
- ¼ cup heavy whipping cream
- 4 large eggs

**Instructions**:

1. Bring a pot of salted water to boil then add the potatoes.
2. Boil the potatoes for 3 to 4 minutes until just tender then drain and set aside.
3. Place the corned beef in a food processor and pulse several times to chop.
4. Heat the oil in a large skillet over medium-high heat.
5. Add the onion and cook for 5 to 6 minutes until tender.
6. Stir in the diced potatoes and cook for another 5 minutes.
7. Add the corned beef then season with salt and pepper to taste.

## Chapter Seven: Muscle-Building Recipes for Bulking

8. Stir in the cream and cook for 1 minute more.
9. Use a spoon to make four depressions in the corned beef mixture and crack an egg into each.
10. Cook for 5 minutes on low heat, covered, until the eggs are cooked to the desired level.

# Chapter Seven: Muscle-Building Recipes for Bulking

## Easy Spanish Omelet

**Servings**: 4

**Ingredients**:

- ¼ cup olive oil
- 1 lbs. new potatoes, peeled and sliced
- 1 medium white onion, chopped
- 2 to 3 tablespoons fresh chopped parsley
- Salt and pepper to taste
- 6 large eggs, beaten well

**Instructions**:

1. Heat the oil in a large skillet over medium heat.
2. Add the potatoes and onion and cook for 30 minutes, partially covered, stirring occasionally.
3. Once the onions and potatoes are very tender, spoon them off into a bowl using a slotted spoon.
4. Heat a medium skillet over medium heat with some of the oil from the other skillet.
5. Beat the eggs with the parsley, salt and pepper then stir in the potato onion mixture.
6. Pour the mixture into the skillet and cook until the eggs are almost set.
7. Flip the omelet and cook until the eggs are set then serve hot.

# Chapter Seven: Muscle-Building Recipes for Bulking

**Sausage and Egg Breakfast Casserole**

**Servings**: 8 to 12

**Ingredients**:

- 10 large eggs, beaten well
- 2 cups fat-free milk
- ½ tablespoons Dijon mustard
- Salt and pepper to taste
- 1 ½ cups shredded cheddar cheese
- 1 lbs. Italian pork sausage
- 2 cups white bread cubes

**Instructions**:

1. Grease a 9x13-inch glass baking dish with cooking spray.
2. Beat the eggs together with the milk, mustard and salt in a mixing bowl.
3. Stir in the cheese and sausage then fold in the bread cubes.
4. Pour into the baking dish then cover and chill overnight.
5. Preheat the oven to 350°F and let the casserole rest at room temperature for 30 minutes.
6. Bake for 30 to 40 minutes until the center is set and a knife inserted in the middle comes out clean.
7. Let rest for 10 minutes before slicing to serve.

## Apple Cinnamon Breakfast Quinoa

**Servings**: 4

**Ingredients**:

- ¾ cups water
- ¾ cups fat-free milk
- ½ teaspoon ground cinnamon
- ½ teaspoon vanilla extract
- ¾ cups uncooked quinoa, rinsed well
- 2 small ripe apples, peeled, cored and chopped

**Instructions**:

1. Whisk together the water, milk, vanilla extract and cinnamon in a small saucepan.
2. Bring the mixture to boil then stir in the quinoa.
3. Cover and simmer on medium-low for 15 minutes until the quinoa absorbs the water.
4. Fluff the quinoa with a fork then spoon into bowls.
5. Top the quinoa with fresh chopped apples to serve.

## Chapter Seven: Muscle-Building Recipes for Bulking

### Ham and Cheese Egg Muffins

**Servings**: 12

**Ingredients**:

- 12 large eggs, beaten well
- ½ cup fat-free milk
- 2 green onions, sliced thin
- Salt and pepper to taste
- 1 ½ cups diced ham
- 1 cup shredded cheddar cheese

**Instructions**:

1. Preheat the oven to 350°F and grease a muffin pan with cooking spray.
2. Beat together the eggs and milk until frothy then stir in the green onions, salt and pepper.
3. Divide the ham among the muffin cups then pour in the egg mixture, filling the cups almost full.
4. Top the egg mixture with cheese then bake for 25 to 30 minutes until the eggs are set.
5. Let the egg muffins cool for 5 minutes before removing from the muffin pan to serve.

Chapter Seven: Muscle-Building Recipes for Bulking

## *2. Snacks and Protein Shakes*

### **Recipes Included in this Section**:

Avocado Deviled Eggs

Tropical Fruit Protein Shake

Cottage Cheese Veggie Dip

Peanut Butter Banana Protein Shake

Spiced Mixed Nuts

Chocolate Covered Strawberry Shake

Peanut Butter Protein Cookies

Berries and Cream Protein Shake

# Chapter Seven: Muscle-Building Recipes for Bulking

**Avocado Deviled Eggs**

**Servings**: 12

**Ingredients**:

- 12 large eggs
- 1 medium avocado, pitted and chopped
- ½ cup olive oil mayonnaise
- 2 tablespoons fresh lemon juice
- 1 tablespoon Dijon mustard
- 1 teaspoon fresh lemon zest
- Salt and pepper to taste

**Instructions**:

1. Bring a large saucepan of water to boil then add the eggs.
2. Reduce heat and boil slowly for 10 minutes then drain and transfer the eggs to a bowl of cold water.
3. When the eggs are cool, remove the shells and cut them in half.
4. Scoop the egg yolks into a food processor then add the remaining ingredients (aside from the egg yolks).
5. Arrange the egg yolk halves upright on a serving dish.
6. Blend the mixture in the food processor until smooth then spoon into a plastic freezer bag.
7. Snip off the corner of the bag then pipe the egg yolk mixture into the egg whites and serve.

## Tropical Fruit Protein Shake

**Servings**: 1

**Ingredients**:

- ½ cup frozen chopped pineapple
- ½ cup frozen chopped mango
- ½ small frozen banana, peeled and sliced
- 1 cup coconut water
- ½ cup ice cubes
- 1 teaspoon coconut extract
- 2 scoops vanilla whey protein powder

**Instructions**:

1. Combine all of the ingredients in a high-speed blender.
2. Pulse the ingredients several times to chop.
3. Blend on high speed for 30 to 60 seconds until smooth.
4. Pour into a glass and enjoy immediately.

## Chapter Seven: Muscle-Building Recipes for Bulking

**Cottage Cheese Veggie Dip**

**Servings**: 4

**Ingredients**:

- 2 cups low-fat cottage cheese
- 1 tablespoon fresh lemon juice
- 1 tablespoon fresh chopped chives
- 1 teaspoon Dijon mustard
- Salt and pepper to taste
- Sliced veggies

**Instructions**:

1. Combine the cottage cheese, lemon juice, chives and Dijon mustard in a food processor.
2. Season with salt and pepper to taste.
3. Pulse the mixture until well combined then spoon into a bowl.
4. Serve with sliced veggies for dipping.

# Chapter Seven: Muscle-Building Recipes for Bulking

## Peanut Butter Banana Protein Shake

**Servings**: 1

**Ingredients**:

- 1 small frozen banana, peeled and sliced
- 2 tablespoons all-natural peanut butter
- 1 cup fat-free milk
- ½ cup fat-free yogurt
- 2 scoops plain or vanilla protein powder

**Instructions**:

1. Combine all of the ingredients in a high-speed blender.
2. Pulse the ingredients several times to chop.
3. Blend on high speed for 30 to 60 seconds until smooth.
4. Pour into a glass and enjoy immediately.

# Chapter Seven: Muscle-Building Recipes for Bulking

## Spiced Mixed Nuts

**Servings**: 8 to 10

**Ingredients**:

- 1 cup whole almonds
- 1 cup raw cashews
- 1 cup whole pecans
- 2 ½ tablespoons coconut oil
- ½ tablespoon chili powder
- ¼ teaspoon ground cumin
- ¼ teaspoon cayenne
- Salt and pepper to taste

**Instructions**:

1. Preheat the oven to 300°F.
2. Combine the nuts in a large mixing bowl.
3. Melt the coconut oil in a small saucepan over medium heat.
4. Stir in the chili powder, cumin and cayenne.
5. Season with salt and pepper to taste and cook for about 20 seconds.
6. Pour the spiced oil over the nuts and toss to coat.
7. Spread the nuts on a parchment-lined baking sheet in a single layer.
8. Bake for 15 to 20 minutes until toasted then serve the nuts warm.

## Chapter Seven: Muscle-Building Recipes for Bulking

### Chocolate Covered Strawberry Shake

**Servings**: 1

**Ingredients**:

- 1 cup frozen sliced strawberries
- 1 cup fat-free milk
- ½ cup fat-free yogurt, plain
- 2 scoops chocolate whey protein powder

**Instructions**:

1. Combine all of the ingredients in a high-speed blender.
2. Pulse the ingredients several times to chop.
3. Blend on high speed for 30 to 60 seconds until smooth.
4. Pour into a glass and enjoy immediately.

# Chapter Seven: Muscle-Building Recipes for Bulking

## Peanut Butter Protein Cookies

**Servings**: about 2 dozen

**Ingredients**:

- 2 cups all-natural peanut butter
- 1 ¼ cups coconut sugar
- 1 cup plain or vanilla protein powder
- 2 large eggs, beaten well

**Instructions**:

1. Preheat the oven to 350°F and line two baking sheets with parchment paper.
2. Combine the peanut butter, sugar, protein powder and egg in a mixing bowl.
3. Whisk until smooth and well combined.
4. Pinch off pieces of dough (about two tablespoons) and roll them into balls by hand.
5. Gently flatten the dough balls with your hands and place them on the baking sheets, spacing them about 1 inch apart.
6. Use a fork to make crisscross markings on the top of each cookie.
7. Bake for 10 to 12 minutes until the edges are just browned.
8. Cool for 2 to 3 minutes on the baking sheet then transfer to wire racks to cool completely.

## Berries and Cream Protein Shake

**Servings**: 1

**Ingredients**:

- ½ cup frozen sliced strawberries
- ¼ cup frozen raspberries
- ¼ cup frozen blueberries
- 1 ½ cups fat-free milk
- ½ cup fat-free yogurt
- 4 to 5 ice cubes
- 2 scoops vanilla whey protein powder

**Instructions**:

1. Combine all of the ingredients in a high-speed blender.
2. Pulse the ingredients several times to chop.
3. Blend on high speed for 30 to 60 seconds until smooth.
4. Pour into a glass and enjoy immediately.

Chapter Seven: Muscle-Building Recipes for Bulking

## 3. Entrée Recipes

### Recipes Included in this Section:

Rosemary Roasted Chicken Breasts

Curried Red Lentil Stew

Coconut-Crusted Halibut Fillets

Soy-Marinated Flank Steak

Spicy Beef and Double Bean Chili

Apple-Roasted Turkey Breast

## Rosemary Roasted Chicken Breasts

**Servings**: 6

**Ingredients**:

- 6 garlic cloves, peeled and minced
- ½ teaspoon salt
- 1 teaspoon dried rosemary
- ¼ teaspoon dried oregano
- Salt and pepper to taste
- 6 boneless skinless chicken breast halves

**Instructions**:

1. Preheat the oven to 500°F.
2. Combine the garlic and salt in a small bowl then mash into a paste with a fork.
3. Stir in the rosemary and oregano then season with salt and pepper to taste.
4. Use a sharp knife to slice a gash into the side of each chicken breast and fill it with ½ teaspoon of the garlic rosemary mixture.
5. Spread the remaining garlic rosemary mixture on top of the chicken breasts.
6. Place the chicken breasts in a shallow baking pan lined with foil.
7. Roast for 20 to 25 minutes until cooked through.

# Chapter Seven: Muscle-Building Recipes for Bulking

## Curried Red Lentil Stew

**Servings**: 6

**Ingredients**:

- 2 tablespoons olive oil
- 1 large yellow onion, chopped
- 1 tablespoon minced garlic
- 1 tablespoon fresh grated ginger
- 6 tablespoons water
- ½ tablespoon curry powder
- ½ teaspoon ground cumin
- ½ teaspoon ground turmeric
- 1 cup uncooked red lentils, stirred well
- 5 cups low-sodium vegetable broth
- 2 medium sweet potatoes, peeled and chopped
- 4 medium carrots, peeled and chopped

**Instructions**:

1. Heat the oil in a large saucepan over medium heat.
2. Add the onion and cook for 6 to 8 minutes until tender.
3. Combine the garlic, ginger and water in a food processor and blend until pureed.
4. Stir the mixture into the saucepan and cook for 5 minutes.

5. Add the curry powder, cumin and turmeric then cook for 1 minute until fragrant.
6. Stir in the lentils and vegetable broth then simmer, covered, for 25 to 30 minutes until very tender.
7. Add the sweet potatoes and carrots then simmer for another 12 to 15 minutes until tender.
8. Adjust seasonings to taste and serve hot.

## Chapter Seven: Muscle-Building Recipes for Bulking

### Coconut-Crusted Halibut Fillets

**Servings**: 4

**Ingredients**:

- 4 (6-ounce) boneless halibut fillets
- Salt and pepper to taste
- 1 large egg, beaten well
- 1 cup unsweetened shredded coconut
- Lemon wedges

**Instructions**:

1. Preheat the oven to 375°F and line a baking sheet with parchment.
2. Rinse the fillets in cold water then pat dry and season with salt and pepper to taste.
3. Beat the egg in a shallow dish and dip each fillet then turn to coat.
4. Dredge the fillets in the shredded coconut then place them on the baking sheet.
5. Bake for 12 to 15 minutes until the flesh flakes easily with a fork.
6. Serve hot with lemon wedges.

## Chapter Seven: Muscle-Building Recipes for Bulking

### Soy-Marinated Flank Steak

**Servings**: 6 to 8

**Ingredients**:

- 1 cup low-sodium soy sauce
- ¼ cup raw honey
- 3 tablespoons rice vinegar
- 1 tablespoon Worcestershire sauce
- Salt and pepper to taste
- 2 lbs. boneless flank steak

**Instructions**:

1. Whisk together all of the ingredients except for the flank steak in a small bowl.
2. Trim the fat then place steak in a shallow dish.
3. Pour the marinade over the steak, turning to coat.
4. Cover the dish and chill for 2 hours, turning every 30 minutes.
5. Preheat the grill to high heat and brush the grates with olive oil.
6. Place the steak on the grill and cook for 6 minutes then brush with glaze.
7. Turn the steak and brush with glaze then grill for another 5 to 6 minutes.
8. Transfer the steak to a cutting board and let rest for 10 minutes before slicing to serve.

# Chapter Seven: Muscle-Building Recipes for Bulking

**Spicy Beef and Double Bean Chili**

**Servings**: 6 to 8

**Ingredients**:

- 1 tablespoon olive oil
- 1 lbs. lean ground beef
- 1 large yellow onion, chopped
- 1 medium red pepper, cored and chopped
- 1 jalapeno, seeded and minced
- 1 teaspoon minced garlic
- 1 tablespoon chili powder
- ¼ teaspoon cayenne
- Salt and pepper to taste
- 1 cup dry red wine
- 1 (15-ounce) can diced tomatoes
- 1 (15-ounce) can red kidney beans, rinsed and drained
- 1 (15-ounce) can pinto beans, rinsed and drained

**Instructions**:

1. Heat the oil in a large saucepan over medium heat.
2. Add the beef and cook until evenly browned.
3. Drain the fat then stir in the onion, red pepper, jalapeno and garlic.
4. Cook for 6 to 8 minutes until tender then stir in the chili powder, cayenne, salt and pepper.

5. Stir in the red wine and cook until the liquid is reduced by half.
6. Add the tomatoes then bring the mixture to a boil and stir in the beans and cooked beef.
7. Simmer on low heat for 1 hour until thick and hot.

## Chapter Seven: Muscle-Building Recipes for Bulking

**Apple-Roasted Turkey Breast**

**Servings**: 4 to 6

**Ingredients**:

- 3 cups apple cider
- 1 cup unsweetened cranberry juice
- ½ cup coarse salt
- 4 tablespoons brown sugar, packed
- Pepper to taste
- 8 cups cold water
- 4 - 4 ½ lbs. bone-in turkey breast
- Olive oil, as needed

**Instructions**:

1. Whisk together the apple cider, cranberry juice, salt, brown sugar, and pepper in a small saucepan
2. Bring to a simmer then cook for 30 to 40 minutes until fragrant.
3. Whisk in the ice water until well combined.
4. Place the turkey breast in a bowl and pour the mixture over it then cover and chill for 4 hours.
5. Preheat the oven to 350°F then remove the turkey from the bowl and pat dry.
6. Place the turkey breast skin-side up in a roasting pan and rub with olive oil.

7. Season with salt and pepper to taste then roast for 1 hour and 30 to 40 minutes until the internal temperature reaches 160°F – brush with glaze every 20 minutes.
8. Transfer the turkey to a cutting board and let rest for 10 minutes before slicing.

# Conclusion

Hopefully by now you understand that bodybuilding doesn't have to mean spending hours in the gym every day, eating nothing but chicken breast and brown rice. Being a bodybuilder is something anyone can achieve - it simply involves making an effort to improve your body through the basic principles of fitness and nutrition. In reading this book you have learned the basics about bodybuilding including what it is and which programs are the most popular. You are also now equipped with the information you need to create your own plans for bulking and cutting so you can achieve your individual bodybuilding goals. By

# Conclusion

using the information in this book you can get started as a bodybuilder and see your body transform as you make changes to your routine. Having the ability to change yourself is extremely empowering, even if you never achieve a Schwarzenegger-like physique.

So, if you are ready to become a bodybuilder then put the information in this book to work! With a little time and determination, you will be amazed at what you can achieve.

# Index

## 5

| | |
|---|---|
| 5x5 Program | 3, 20 |

## A

| | |
|---|---|
| activity | 12, 33, 36, 38, 41, 42, 47 |
| adrenaline | 33 |
| American Dietetic Association | 42 |
| amino acids | 53 |
| anxiety | 14 |
| Arnold Schwarzenegger | 18 |
| arthritis | 14 |

## B

| | |
|---|---|
| back | 10, 16, 22, 27, 49 |
| banned | 19 |
| barbell | 10, 11 |
| beginners | 20, 27 |
| bench | 9, 11 |
| benefits | 8, 12, 13, 15 |
| biceps | 22, 27 |
| blood | 10, 14, 24 |
| body | 2, 7, 9, 10, 13, 14, 15, 16, 17, 22, 23, 24, 25, 26, 27, 28, 29, 32, 34, 36, 40, 42, 45, 46, 47, 48, 49, 50, 53, 54, 55, 56, 58, 59, 60, 61, 63, 115 |
| body composition | 7, 16, 40, 47 |
| body type | 46, 47 |
| bodybuilder | 2, 7, 12, 13, 18, 22, 27, 36, 42, 50, 115, 116 |
| bodyweight | 9, 11, 29, 30, 31, 39, 41, 53, 63 |
| bones | 14 |

| | |
|---|---|
| brain | 14 |
| breakfast | 64 |
| bulking | 2, 8, 34, 35, 36, 37, 38, 39, 43, 45, 46, 49, 55, 115 |

## C

| | |
|---|---|
| calorie | 10, 30, 31, 35, 36, 37, 38, 39, 40, 41, 42, 43, 45, 47, 49, 50, 52, 53, 56, 58, 64, 125 |
| carbohydrate | 29, 30, 31, 45, 47, 49, 53, 56, 57, 60, 63 |
| cardiac muscle | 24 |
| cardiovascular | 14, 36, 38 |
| chemical | 9 |
| chest | 9, 10, 22, 27 |
| cholesterol | 14, 57 |
| cognitive performance | 14 |
| competition | 11, 17, 18, 19, 36 |
| compound exercises | 22, 27 |
| confidence | 14 |
| control | 24, 25, 37 |
| curls | 11 |
| cutting | 2, 8, 34, 35, 36, 37, 38, 39, 43, 45, 46, 49, 50, 51, 55, 64, 110, 114, 115 |

## D

| | |
|---|---|
| deadlifts | 11 |
| deficit | 38, 39, 44, 49, 50, 56, 58, 125 |
| definition | 7, 13 |
| depression | 14 |
| dumbbells | 7, 17 |

## E

| | |
|---|---|
| eat | 2, 7, 8, 15, 21, 31, 34, 49, 50, 55, 56, 57, 59, 60, 63, 64 |
| ectomorph | 46 |

| | |
|---|---|
| endomorph | 46 |
| endurance | 13, 14 |
| energy | 10, 28, 29, 31, 32, 34, 45, 53, 56, 60 |
| Eugen Sandow | 17 |
| exercise | 8, 9, 10, 11, 13, 14, 17, 21 |

## F

| | |
|---|---|
| fat | 9, 10, 13, 15, 28, 29, 31, 35, 36, 37, 38, 39, 42, 43, 45, 46, 47, 48, 49, 50, 51, 52, 54, 55, 57, 58, 60, 64, 69, 72, 74, 75, 76, 77, 78, 79, 81, 84, 93, 94, 95, 99, 100, 102, 104, 110, 111, 125 |
| fatty acids | 31 |
| fitness | 2, 7, 13, 15, 22, 115 |
| flexibility | 21 |
| Franco Columbu | 18 |
| FST-7 Program | 3, 20, 21 |
| fuel | 15, 28, 30, 32, 45, 48, 53, 54, 60, 61, 63 |
| Full Body Workout Program | 3, 20, 22 |

## G

| | |
|---|---|
| German Volume Training | 3, 20, 21 |
| goals | 8, 13, 23, 35, 37, 38, 39, 115 |
| gym | 2, 13, 24, 115 |

## H

| | |
|---|---|
| healthy | 12, 13, 14, 30, 49, 51, 53, 64 |
| heart | 10, 14, 24 |
| heartrate | 33 |
| history | 12 |
| hormone balance | 29 |
| hormones | 26, 32 |
| hyperplasia | 25 |

| | |
|---|---|
| hypertrophy | 25 |

## I

| | |
|---|---|
| injury | 14, 33 |
| intake | 10, 30, 31, 35, 36, 37, 38, 41, 42, 43, 47, 49, 52, 53, 58, 64 |
| involuntary | 24 |
| isolated | 20, 27 |

## J

| | |
|---|---|
| joints | 14 |

## K

| | |
|---|---|
| knees | 11 |

## L

| | |
|---|---|
| lean | 9, 13, 15, 29, 30, 31, 39, 42, 43, 46, 49, 52, 53, 60, 63, 64, 84, 111 |
| leg | 11, 22 |
| lifting | 9, 10, 12, 13, 15, 16, 26, 27 |

## M

| | |
|---|---|
| macronutrient | 28, 29, 31, 36, 37, 38, 39, 45, 46, 47, 57 |
| macronutrient ratios | 28, 31, 36, 37, 39, 45, 46, 47 |
| maintain | 26, 31, 39, 40, 43, 46, 49, 51, 53 |
| mass | 13, 15, 29, 38, 39, 42, 43, 45, 46, 49, 125, 126 |
| meals | 31, 34, 49, 54 |
| mesomorph | 46 |
| Mifflin-St. Jeor Equation | 41, 42 |
| minerals | 29, 58 |

| | |
|---|---|
| mistakes | 35, 36, 38, 48, 55 |
| mood | 14 |
| muscle | 7, 9, 10, 11, 13, 15, 18, 20, 21, 22, 24, 25, 26, 27, 28, 29, 31, 32, 34, 35, 36, 37, 38, 39, 42, 43, 45, 46, 47, 48, 49, 50, 52, 53, 54, 55, 56, 58, 59, 63, 124, 125, 126 |
| muscle groups | 20, 21, 22, 27 |
| myths | 48, 55, 124 |

## N

| | |
|---|---|
| neurons | 25 |
| neurotransmitters | 27 |
| nutrients | 28 |
| nutrition | 2, 8, 14, 15, 23, 27, 28, 29, 31, 48, 52, 55, 59, 60, 61, 115, 125, 126 |

## O

| | |
|---|---|
| omega-3 | 31 |
| omega-6 | 31 |
| oxygen | 9, 14 |

## P

| | |
|---|---|
| percentage | 9, 13, 15, 42, 43 |
| physical training | 10 |
| physique | 13, 16, 116 |
| post-workout | 59, 63 |
| powerlifting | 11 |
| pre-workout | 60 |
| principles | 2, 8, 23, 34, 36, 39, 115 |
| programs | 2, 8, 12, 20, 21, 23, 27, 115, 124 |
| proportions | 17 |
| protein | 26, 28, 29, 30, 31, 34, 39, 45, 49, 50, 52, 53, 54, 57, 58, 60, 61, 63, 64, 98, 100, 102, 103, 104 |

| | |
|---|---|
| protein shakes | 53 |
| protein synthesis | 26 |
| pulse | 10, 76, 90 |
| push-ups | 11 |

# R

| | |
|---|---|
| recipes | 8, 64 |
| refeeding | 59 |
| rep | 10 |
| repetitions | 11, 20, 21, 22, 26 |
| resistance | 11 |
| rest | 11, 21, 23, 32, 33, 93, 110, 114, 125 |
| running | 9, 10 |

# S

| | |
|---|---|
| sarcomere | 25 |
| sarcoplasmic | 25 |
| saturated | 30, 56 |
| schedule | 22, 33, 34 |
| self-esteem | 14 |
| set | 10, 11, 13, 20, 21, 51, 66, 71, 76, 78, 90, 92, 93, 95 |
| Sir Arthur Conan Doyle | 17 |
| Sir Charles Lawes | 17 |
| size | 10, 20, 22, 24, 25, 26, 31 |
| skeletal muscle | 24 |
| skin | 7, 10, 113 |
| sleep | 32, 33, 34, 50 |
| slow-digesting | 30, 53, 56, 60 |
| smoothies | 64 |
| snacks | 64 |
| sport | 13, 19 |
| sports drinks | 54 |

| | |
|---|---:|
| squats | 11 |
| steroid | 18 |
| strength | 14, 16, 17, 20, 22, 26, 27, 33 |
| stress | 14, 26 |
| stronger | 25 |
| strongmen | 16, 17 |
| surplus | 37, 38, 45, 56 |

## T

| | |
|---|---:|
| tension | 17 |
| testosterone | 9, 26, 32, 53 |
| tips | 2, 8, 23, 29, 31, 33, 35, 37, 39, 48, 49, 51, 52, 54, 55, 59 |
| training | 11, 12, 15, 18, 21, 22, 23, 24, 26, 27, 30, 33 |

## U

| | |
|---|---:|
| unsaturated | 30 |
| Upper/Lower Split Training | 3, 20, 22 |

## V

| | |
|---|---:|
| veins | 7 |

## W

| | |
|---|---|
| water | 50, 62, 67, 70, 79, 81, 82, 85, 90, 94, 97, 98, 107, 109, 113 |
| water retention | 50 |
| weight | 9, 10, 11, 12, 13, 16, 20, 26, 29, 35, 36, 37, 38, 39, 40, 42, 43, 46, 47, 51, 56, 57, 58, 60, 125 |
| workout | 10, 15, 21, 22, 25, 27, 32, 33, 50, 53, 54, 56, 59, 60, 61, 63, 125, 126 |

Diet and Nutrition for Bodybuilding

# References

"3 Keys to Dialing in Your Macronutrient Ratios." Bodybuilding.com. <http://www.bodybuilding.com/fun/macro-math-3-keys-to-dialing-in-your-macro-ratios.html>

"5 Best Bodybuilding Programs to Pack on Serious Muscle." Bodybuilding.com. <http://www.bodybuilding.com/fun/5-best-bodybuilding-programs.htm>

"8 Nutritional Myths Debunked." Bodybuilding.com. <http://www.bodybuilding.com/fun/fact-or-fiction-8-nutritional-myths-debunked.html>

"10 Nutritional Commandments for Cutting." Bodybuilding.com. <http://www.bodybuilding.com/fun/catcommand2.htm>

"A List of the Best Weight Training Exercises for Each Muscle Group." A Workout Routine. <http://www.aworkoutroutine.com/list-of-exercises-for-each-muscle-group/>

"An Introduction to Bodybuilding." Weight Loss for All. <http://www.weightlossforall.com/bodybuilding.htm>

"Bodybuilding Basic Principles." Bodybuilding.com. <http://www.bodybuilding.com/fun/doyon1.htm>

"Bulking and Cutting – How to Bulk Up & Cut for More Muscle/Less Fat." A Workout Routine. <http://www.aworkoutroutine.com/bulk-and-cut/>

"Calorie Deficit to Lose Weight – Setting Your Calorie Intake for Weight Loss." A Calorie Counter. <http://www.acaloriecounter.com/diet/calorie-deficit-to-lose-weight/>

"Calorie Maintenance Level – Daily Calorie Requirements Calculator." A Calorie Counter. <http://www.acaloriecounter.com/diet/calorie-maintenance-calculator-daily-calorie-requirements/>

"Eat While You Lift." Muscle and Fitness. <http://www.muscleandfitness.com/nutrition/gain-mass/eating-while-you-lift>

"How to Gain Muscle Without Gaining Fat." A Workout Routine. <http://www.aworkoutroutine.com/how-to-gain-muscle-without-gaining-fat/>

"Hunter Labrada's Guide to Pre-Workout Nutrition and Supplementation." Bodybuilding.com. <http://www.bodybuilding.com/fun/hunter-labradas-guide-pre-workout-nutrition-supplementation.html>

"Importance of Rest and Recovery in Muscle Building." 2 Build Muscle Fast. <http://www.2buildmusclefast.com/2011/01/importance-of-rest-and-recovery-in.html>

Leyva, John. "How Do Muscles Grow? The Science of Muscle Growth." Built Lean. <http://www.builtlean.com/2013/09/17/muscles-grow/>

"Macronutrients: The Importance of Carbohydrate, Protein and Fat." McKinley Health Center. <http://www.mckinley.illinois.edu/handouts/macronutrients.htm

"Muscle Food: 10 Nutrition Rules to Build Muscle." Muscle & Fitness. <http://www.muscleandfitness.com/nutrition/gain-mass/muscle-food-10-nutrition-rules-build-muscle>

"Muscular System." Inner Body. <http://www.innerbody.com/image/musfov.html>

"Pre and Post Workout Meal – What to Eat Before and After Working Out." A Calorie Counter. <http://www.acaloriecounter.com/diet/pre-and-post-workout-meal/>

South, Clayton. "The Principles of Bodybuilding." Bodybuilding.com. <http://www.bodybuilding.com/fun/south41.htm>

"What is Bodybuilding? Overall Benefits Are Absolutely Amazing!" Bodybuilding.com. <http://www.bodybuilding.com/fun/what_is_bodybuilding.htm>

"What's the Significance of the Big 3 Exercises?" Bodybuilding.com. <http://www.bodybuilding.com/fun/topicoftheweek49.htm>

## More Titles available…

Feeding Baby
Cynthia Cherry
978-1941070000

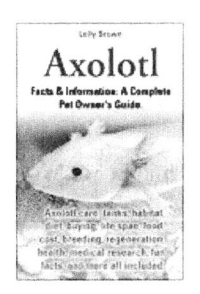

Axolotl
Lolly Brown
978-0989658430

Dysautonomia, POTS Syndrome
Frederick Earlstein
978-0989658485

Degenerative Disc Disease Explained
Frederick Earlstein
978-0989658485

Diet and Nutrition for Bodybuilding

More Titles available…

Sinusitis, Hay Fever,
Allergic Rhinitis Explained
Frederick Earlstein
978-1941070024

Wicca
Riley Star
978-1941070130

Zombie Apocalypse
Rex Cutty
978-1941070154

Capybara
Lolly Brown
978-1941070062

Diet and Nutrition for Bodybuilding

# More Titles available…

Eels As Pets
Lolly Brown
978-1941070167

Scabies and Lice Explained
Frederick Earlstein
978-1941070017

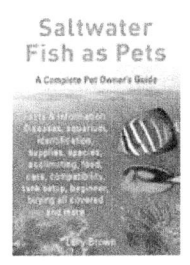

Saltwater Fish As Pets
Lolly Brown
978-0989658461

Torticollis Explained
Frederick Earlstein
978-1941070055

Diet and Nutrition for Bodybuilding

More Titles available…

Kennel Cough
Lolly Brown
978-0989658409

Physiotherapist, Physical Therapist
Christopher Wright
978-0989658492

Rats, Mice, and Dormice As Pets
Lolly Brown
978-1941070079

Wallaby and Wallaroo Care
Lolly Brown
978-1941070031

Diet and Nutrition for Bodybuilding

# More Titles available…

Bodybuilding Supplements Explained
Jon Shelton
978-1941070239

Demonology
Riley Star
978-19401070314

Pigeon Racing
Lolly Brown
978-1941070307

Dwarf Hamster
Lolly Brown
978-1941070390

Diet and Nutrition for Bodybuilding

More Titles available…

Cryptozoology
Rex Cutty
978-1941070406

Eye Strain
Frederick Earlstein
978-1941070369

Inez The Miniature Elephant
Asher Ray
978-1941070353

Vampire Apocalypse
Rex Cutty
978-1941070321

Diet and Nutrition for Bodybuilding